Hampton National Historic Site

A PICTORIAL GLIMPSE OF MARYLAND LIFE
1783–1948

View of the Mansion from the Lower House
(BV)

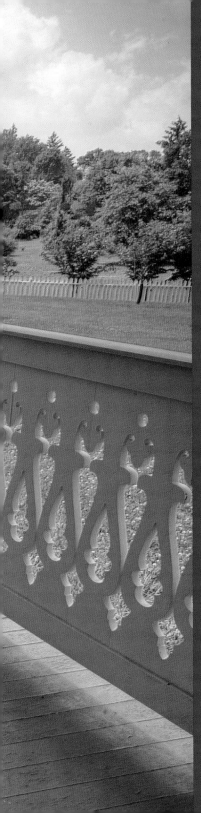

Historic Hampton, Inc.

presents

Hampton National Historic Site

A PICTORIAL GLIMPSE OF MARYLAND LIFE
1783–1948

PHOTOGRAPHERS
TIM ERVIN
BARBARA VIETZKE

EDITOR
EILEEN KALINOSKI

THE
DONNING COMPANY
PUBLISHERS

The Donning Company Publishers
184 Business Park Drive, Suite 206
Virginia Beach, VA 23462

Steve Mull, *General Manager*
Barbara B. Buchanan, *Office Manager*
Richard A. Horwege, *Senior Editor*
Stephanie Danko, *Graphic Designer*
Derek Eley, *Imaging Artist*
Lori Porter, *Project Research Coordinator*
Tonya Hannink, *Marketing Specialist*
Pamela Engelhard, *Marketing Advisor*

Dennis N. Walton, *Project Director*

Library of Congress Cataloging-in-Publication Data

Vietzke, Barbara.
    Hampton National Historic Site : a pictorial glimpse of Maryland life, 1783–1948 / editor, Eileen Kalinoski ; photographers, Barbara Vietzke, Tim Ervin.
        p.   cm.
    ISBN 978-1-57864-618-0 (hard cover : alk. paper)
1. Hampton National Historic Site (Md.)—Pictorial works. 2. Seasons—Maryland—Hampton National Historic Site—Pictorial works. 3. Natural history—Maryland—Hampton National Historic Site—Pictorial works. 4. Historic buildings—Maryland—Towson—Pictorial works. 5. Interior decoration—Maryland—Towson—Pictorial works. 6. House furnishings—Maryland—Towson—Pictorial works. 7. Towson (Md.)—Social life and customs—Pictorial works. 8. Maryland—Social life and customs—Pictorial works. I. Ervin, Tim. II. Kalinoski, Eileen. III. Title.
    F187.B2V54 2010
    975.2'71—dc22
                                                                        2010007632

Printed in the USA at Walsworth Publishing Company

(TE)

(BV)

DEDICATION

Historic Hampton, Inc., is blessed by many hardworking volunteers. This book was produced entirely by volunteers. Barbara Vietzke and Tim Ervin have devoted hundreds of hours traveling, photographing, and processing these stunning photographs. Historic Hampton, Inc., the park's primary friend's group is extremely grateful to Barbara and Tim for sharing their talent.

A special debt of gratitude is owed to Rhoda Dorsey, who has been a constant champion of Hampton since 1952, and still provides cheer and invaluable advice to us all.

Finally, we want to thank all of our dedicated volunteers and contributors, including members of the Federated Garden Clubs of Maryland; the Women's Committee of Historic Hampton; the Colonial Dames of America, Chapter I; and innumerable others who make Hampton National Historic Site the showplace that it is today.

ACKNOWLEDGMENTS

The wonderful landscapes and historic building in this book are lovingly preserved through the tireless support of the members of the National Park Service. Historic Hampton, Inc., wishes to thank Gay Vietzke, Superintendent; Vince Vaise, Chief of Interpretation; Paul Bitzel, Cultural Resources Manager; Wayne Boyd, Chief of Maintenance; Gregory Weidman, Curator; Debbie Patterson, Registrar; Cora Provins, Museum Technician; Telia Shipowick, Museum Technician; Rangers William Curtis, Kirby Shedlowski, Angela Roberts-Burton, Alan Gephardt, Carol Van Natta, and Laura Marshallsay.

NOTE: Most photos are marked with the initials of the photographer who produced the photo: TE for Tim Ervin; BV for Barbara Vietzke. The image on the front dust jacket was taken by Tim Ervin, the back dust jacket by Barbara Vietzke.

(BV)

Contents

(TE)

(BV)

HAMPTON IN AUTUMN

HAMPTON IN WINTER

Foggy morning
(TE)

Preface

This book is an invitation. The photographs presented here showcase both the natural and cultural beauty of the Hampton National Historic Site. From early dawn with the moon on the wane; to the fading streaks of orange and purple at sunset; from the brilliant pinks of the peonies in the garden to the vivid red and gold of the Drawing Room, this book entices the visitor to experience a myriad of color and design. This beauty, however, is not the only reason to visit. Far more significantly, Hampton National Historic Site is a stage for the drama of events personal and national, heroic and tragic, which reveal to modern visitors insights of our national story. The lives of the Ridgleys, an American family, and those who served them, mirror the history of America.

The collections in the Mansion span the globe: there are European and Chinese porcelains; French, English, and American furniture; Italian landscape paintings and American family portraits; and furnishings reflecting Greco-Roman and French influences. At the height of the Ridgely fortunes, the Mansion was filled with the exquisite workmanship of the best artisans of the age. From the delicate rosy flowers on Eliza's pale aqua porcelain jardiniere; to the robust cherub, the graceful mother and child on the porticos, elegance is everywhere. Along with the imported luxury goods, there is also American artistry in the ornamental curves of the sleigh in the stables, and the tiny detailed painted stag on the side of one of the carriages, along with the more prosaic tools used every day such as the saddles and tack, the rustic jugs and simple furniture in the Lower House and Slave Quarters.

Yet among all the beauty, there is another side to this story that these images cannot convey. The realities of everyday life for many at Hampton involved dirt, disease, the extremes of heat and cold; backbreaking work; the terrible injuries and the frequent deaths of children and adults as well as the intense uncertainties of financial panics, riots, and war. Indentured servants, enslaved African-Americans, poor farmers, and wealthy landowners all participated in the American experience that was Hampton.

Hampton National Historic Site offers visitors the unique opportunity to view and experience original objects in their historical context. Over 90 percent of the items on display are original to the Ridgely family. Some things are put away for safekeeping and periodically brought out for display, but most of what you see were actual Ridgely family possessions. Hampton National Historic Site is a priceless historical treasure, the Ridgely family left many records that provide insight into American life for over two hundred years. An online finding aid is available on the National Park Service website. These resources of Maryland and Mid-Atlantic history tell us where we came from and why. And they tell us who we are, so we can move forward with insight and courage.

Unlike many historic sites, no single figure dominates the story. Hampton offers a vivid view into the way people lived: master and slave, indentured servant and paid worker. Hampton is authentic, and the lessons it has to offer are about real Americans. Accept the invitation and explore this special place deemed worthy enough to be owned and maintained by the American people as a unit of the National Park Service. Visitors who are drawn by Hampton's beauty cannot help but be enticed by a deepening fascination for the place and its stories. America's past is here, sustained for the pleasure and contemplation of anyone who cares to see. It is an invitation whose temptations are difficult to resist.

Flag Day Celebration
(TE)

FOREWORD

It is a pleasure to welcome you to this collection of pictures of the Hampton National Historic Site. The site is comprised of two separate properties that hold the Mansion, the gardens and outbuildings, the farm building and Slave Quarters, and a large collection of furniture, textiles, art, music, books, photographs, manuscripts, and all the big and small tools of living that the Ridgely family acquired and treasured over 150 years. With this rich and varied collection, Hampton sheds light on the life of the family and their friends, servants, and slaves. It can thus help us to understand the journey we have made since the founding of our country, and appreciate the importance of preserving and displaying this historical record.

We have other reasons for the importance of Hampton. Efforts to save and preserve the Mansion and estate led directly to the formation of the National Trust for Historic Preservation. Hampton was thus responsible in part for an organization that has had an extraordinary national impact in preserving our past. In addition, recent efforts to conserve and renew the Mansion and the farm property have come about through the active cooperation of the federal government in the person of the National Park Service, the governments of Baltimore County and the State of Maryland, and private citizens enlisted by Historic Hampton, Inc., the voluntary support group devoted to the site. This kind of public-private cooperation is a model of how we may conserve our past for the present and future.

Looking at these photographs of Hampton you will, I hope, appreciate the efforts of all those volunteers who have been so important to Hampton. Please come see what inspired these efforts and enjoy the many delights of this beautiful historic site.

Long a member and past president of the Executive Committee of Historic Hampton, Inc., Rhoda Dorsey is President Emeritus of Goucher College, which is currently located in Towson on property that used to be part of the Hampton Estate.

Stag head gates
(TE)

INTRODUCTION

Still imposing after more than 220 years, the Mansion sits at the end of a grassy vista looking much the same as in 1790 when it was one of the largest private residences in the United States. Hampton and its acres of parkland are preserved along with the Lower House and Slave Quarters and many outbuildings. Whether swathed in morning mists or lit by the setting sun, Hampton offers the visitor a feast of historic delights.

Morning visitors
(TE)

(BV)

Hampton in Spring

Mansion outbuildings
(BV)

(BV)

Paul Bitzel, Cultural Resources Manager

May Garden Party celebrants:
Gregory Weidman, Betti
Sheldon, Mary Arnold,
Catherine Thomas Burnett,
and Ann Boyce

(TE)

Mansion cupola

Slave Quarters circa 1850s

Garden Maintenance Building circa 1880s

(TE)

Parterre 1, Falling Garden

Paris porcelain dessert and cake plates 1834

(BV)

(BV)

Garden peony

Paris porcelain vase circa 1848

(TE)

Unplanted parterre, Falling Garden

Bedchamber chair and detail by Robert Renwick,
Baltimore 1873

23

(BV)

French silver pitcher 1834, English plated silver candelabra
1848, French furnishing fabrics circa 1850

Details of candelabra

(BV)

Rose Canton porcelain relish dish circa 1850
Live roses such as those Eliza Ridgely loved

(TE)

Baltimore painted armchair circa 1810

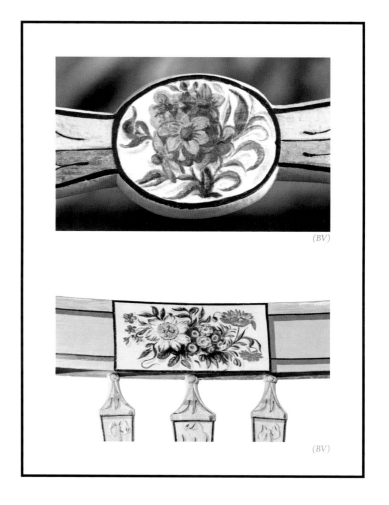

(BV)

(BV)

28

(BV)

(TE)

Chinese rose mandarin porcelain garden seat circa 1840

Paris porcelain cache pot circa 1840

Magnolias

(TE)

(TE)

(TE)

Maryland tall clock circa 1800

(BV)

(BV)

*Windowpane in Master
Bedchamber with signatures
of Ridgely brides*

*Master Bedchamber in spring
furnished to reflect 1790–1810*

(TE)

Hampton in Summer

Carriage gates to the Mansion

Misty summer's day

(TE)

Hampton Dairy milk bottle circa 1920

Stoneware milk pails in the Hampton Dairy

(BV)

(TE)

Living history interpreter during Dairy Day program

The Dairy circa 1790

(TE)

Ranger Robert Stewart

(TE)

Ranger Vince Vaise

Rangers Alan Gebhardt, Vince Vaise, and James Bailey scything at Hay Day

(TE)

Singer Doug Jimerson

*Living history performers
at Second Sunday event
at the Lower House*

(TE)

(BV)

Candle holder in the smithy's fire

Volunteer Jim Maness hard at work during a blacksmithing demonstration

Blacksmithed candle holder

(TE)

David Keltz performs Edgar Allan Poe

Illustration from Ridgely family copy of The Raven

Cover of The Raven

Illustration from The Raven

(TE)

1941 Packard in a July Fourth Parade

Interior of the carriage

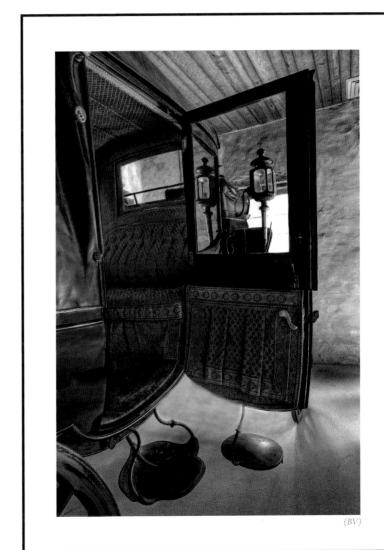

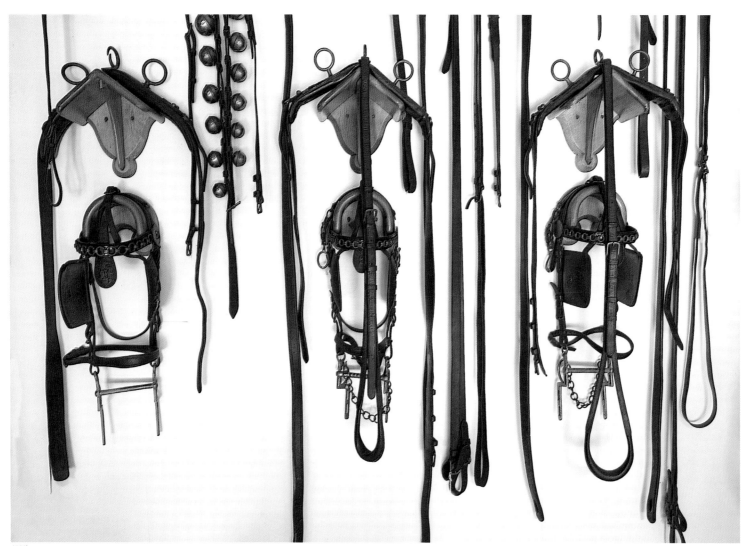

*Assorted horse
tack at the Stables*

*Saddle displayed
in Stable 1*

(BV)

x

55

(BV)

55

(TE)

Bridle

(BV)

Stirrup

56

(TE)

(TE)

(BV)

Carriage detail

Wheel cap

(TE)

Carriage lantern

(TE)

59

(TE)

Carriage horse

Caleche carriage circa 1870

(BV)

Staircase to the cupola at the Hampton Mansion

View from cupola looking toward the Lower House

(BV)

(BV)

Music Room in summer circa 1870–1890

65

Parterre at the Falling Garden

Greenhouse at dawn

(TE)

The cupola at dawn
Field by the Lower House

(TE)

(TE)

Mansion by moonlight

Stable lane

(BV)

Hampton in Autumn

Left: Mule Barn and haystacks

Kitchen hyphen at the Mansion

View from the west portico

Grounds of the Lower House with outbuildings

(TE)

(TE)

Society for the Preservation of
African American Arts Singers

Kitchen pots in the Slave Quarters

Blacksmith's House, late afternoon

(TE) (TE)

Genteel sport circa 1860s

Chesapeake Bay retriever

Country gentlemen, portrayed by Brian Alexander and Jim Bailey

(TE)

Tenant Farmers' Quarters circa 1910

Log cabin near the Lower House

84

(BV)

(TE)

Mule Barn circa 1850

Upper Stables circa 1805

(TE)

(BV)

Autumn view of the Mansion from the Falling Garden

Dew on late bloom in the Falling Garden

Falling Garden by moonlight

(BV)

(TE)

Greenhouse structure

Greenhouse circa 1840s

91

(TE)

(TE)

Living history interpreters at Manly Arts Day

(BV)

(BV)

The Parlour in autumn furnished to reflect 1790–1810

(BV)

(BV)

(BV)

More views of the Parlour

95

(BV)

Carte de visite of Eliza Ridgely circa 1862

*The Great Hall with copy of the
Thomas Sully portrait of Eliza
Eichelberger Ridgely at age sixteen*

(TE)

(BV)

English cut-glass chandelier circa 1790

Chinese export porcelain palace jar circa 1850

*American gilded pier
glass circa 1810*

(BV)

(BV)

Icehouse circa 1790

West lawn of the Mansion

(TE)

(TE)

Dawn's early light in the Falling Garden

Greenhouse at sunset

103

(TE)

Hampton in Winter

(BV)

The family cemetery

(BV)

(BV)

(BV)

(TE)

Yuletide begins

*Sandy Ludwig from "Oh My Heart!
Carriages" leads a winter carriage ride*

(TE)

(BV)

Servants' call bells in the east hyphen

(BV)

(BV)

Bust of Mercury by Wedgwood circa 1820

West portico

(BV)

Lady's riding hat circa 1890

(BV)

Leather hatbox circa 1870

(BV)

Traveling trunk circa 1900

Guest Bedchamber in winter,
furnished to reflect 1890–1910

(BV)

Baltimore low post bed circa 1830

Yuletide decorations in the Tenants' Quarters

(TE)

Chinese lacquered furniture in the Drawing Room circa 1840

(TE)

(TE)

(TE)

(TE)

(TE)

(TE)

The Drawing Room, furnished to reflect 1830–1860

Carpet details

*Reproduction of original
Drawing Room tapestry
velvet carpet circa 1850*

(TE)

More views of the Drawing Room

(TE)

(BV)

(TE)

Detail Baltimore painted side chair by John Finlay 1832

Reproduction of the Drawing Room wallpaper circa 1840

(TE)

(TE)

The Northeast Bedchamber, furnished
to reflect 1840–1860 children's room

Dolls' tea party

Children's gifts at Yuletide

125

Yuletide in the Music Room

Convex Federal mirror reflecting Christmas tree

Children's Yuletide gifts in the Music Room

127

Child's sled

(TE)

(TE)

(BV)

Detail of child's sled

Nineteenth century children's Yuletide gifts

(TE)

129

(TE)   (TE)

The Dining Room furnished to reflect 1810–1830

Portrait of General John Eager Howard by Charles Wilson Peale circa 1785

Side table in the Dining Room set with desserts at Yuletide

The Ridgely family coat of arms and stag's head crest embellishes porcelain and stained glass

(BV)

(TE)

Ridgely family stag's head crest on curtain tie-back and carriage door

A stag on Hampton's property

(BV)

Eliza Ridgely's harp, made by Erard of London, 1817

Parlor games of the nineteenth century

Choreographie Antique performing historic dance

(TE)

(BV)

Detail of the Music Room window shade

Hand-painted shade in the Music Room

Instruments in the the Music Room

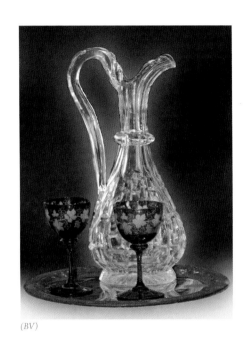

(BV)

(BV)

Wine ewer and glasses circa 1850

German white wine bottle 1868

Decanter and glasses

East view of the Mansion on a winter's evening
(TE)

ABOUT THE EDITOR AND PHOTOGRAPHERS

Eileen Kalinoski, Editor

After her family, Eileen Kalinoski has three major passions in life: her dogs, her oil painting, and Hampton National Historic Site. She conceived of the idea of a coffee table book for Hampton, and then was asked to be editor. After the completion of the book, she looks forward to painting dog portraits, learning to paint landscapes, and continuing to manage the Museum Shop for Hampton.

Tim Ervin, Photographer

Tim Ervin describes himself as an enthusiastic amateur photographer. He photographs events at Fort McHenry National Monument and Historic Shrine and Hampton National Historic Site as part of the Volunteer in Parks Program. Cannon fire, living history, and eagles are favorite subjects. Particular areas he loves are National Parks and Wildlife Refuges. Tim thoroughly relishes capturing images of Hampton, the only National Park preserved for its architectural significance.

Barbara Vietzke, Photographer

Barbara Vietzke, a member of Canon Professional Services and the Photographic Society of America, has been inspired by photographing our National Parks and Historic Sites for many years. A Hampton National Historic Site volunteer, she has been thrilled to explore this exquisite Mansion and estate, seeking to reflect its grandeur whether through the detail of macro or the wonder of a wide-angle lens.